The Lord's Supper

The Lord's Supper

by
John MacArthur, Jr.

WORD OF GRACE COMMUNICATIONS
P.O. Box 4000
Panorama City, CA 91412

© 1987 by
JOHN F. MACARTHUR, JR.

All Scripture quotations, unless noted otherwise, are from the *New Scofield Reference Bible*, King James Version. Copyright © 1967 by Oxford University Press, Inc. Reprinted by permission.

Library of Congress Cataloging in Publication Data

MacArthur, John F.
  The Lord's Supper.

  (Bible studies)
  Includes indexes.
    1. Lord's Supper—Biblical teaching.   2. Bible.   N.T.
  Matthew XXVI, 17-30—Criticism, interpretation, etc.
  3. Bible.   N.T.   Corinthians, 1st XI, 17-34—Criticism,
  interpretation, etc.   I. Title.   II. Series: MacArthur,
  John F.   Bible studies.
  BV823.M24   1987   234'.163   87-20407
  ISBN 0-8024-5310-4

  1 2 3 4 5 6 7 Printing/LC/Year 91 90 89 88 87

Printed in the United States of America

Contents

These Bible studies are taken from messages delivered by Pastor-Teacher John MacArthur, Jr., at Grace Community Church in Panorama City, California. These messages have been combined into a 4-tape album entitled *The Lord's Supper*. You may purchase this series either in an attractive vinyl cassette album or as individual cassettes. To purchase these tapes, request the album *The Lord's Supper*, or ask for the tapes by their individual GC numbers. Please consult the current price list; then, send your order, making your check payable to:

WORD OF GRACE COMMUNICATIONS
P.O. Box 4000
Panorama City, CA 91412

Or call the following toll-free number:
1-800-55-GRACE

1
The Last Passover—Part 1

Outline

Introduction
A. The Theme of Sacrifice
    1. In the Old Testament
    2. In the New Testament
B. The Theme of Matthew's Gospel

Lesson
I. Experiencing the Final Passover (vv. 17-25)
    A. Setting the Time (vv. 17-19)
        1. The persistence
        2. The purpose
            a) The significance of Passover
                (1) The symbol of deliverance
                (2) The slaughter of lambs
            b) The significance of unleavened bread
        3. The preparation
            a) The request of the disciples
            b) The response of Jesus
                (1) The secret preparation
                    (a) The representatives of the Savior
                        i)   The indefinite man
                        ii)   The intimate disciples
                    (b) The reason for the secrecy
                (2) The significant obligation
            c) The reaction of the disciples
        4. The problem
            a) The chronological discrepancy
            b) The consistent proofs

Introduction

The purpose of the earthly life of Jesus Christ was His sacrificial death. He came into the world to die. In Mark 10:45 Jesus says, "Even the Son of man came . . . to give his life a ransom for many." That was not an alteration in the plan; that *was* the plan. It was not a bad ending to a good beginning. Jesus came to die for the sins of the world. One writer has said that the cross was not the end of the story but the theme of the story.

A. The Theme of Sacrifice

    1. In the Old Testament

        The meaning of sacrifice was progressively given by Old Testament revelation. In the story of Adam and Eve we learn that sacrifice is necessary to cover sin (Gen. 3:21). In the sacrifice of Abel we learn that a certain sacrifice is necessary to please God—a sacrifice of death (Gen. 4:4). From Abraham we learn that God will provide that sacrifice, just as He provided an animal in the place of Isaac (Gen. 22:13). The Passover reminds us that the sacrifice must be without spot or blemish (Ex. 12:5). All those aspects of a sacrifice prepare us for Jesus Christ, the ultimate sacrifice.

    2. In the New Testament

        Everything in the New Testament focuses on the cross. Between 20 and 40 percent of the text of the gospels centers on the final week of the Lord's life. The book of Acts is the record of the world's reaction to the death and resurrection of Christ. The epistles were written to those who believe in the death and resurrection of Christ, to instruct them in the implications of it. In the book of Revelation we meet the Lamb that was slain, who will return as King of kings and Lord of lords.

The death of Jesus Christ is the focal point of all redemptive history. It is no accident; it is the apex of the plan of God. From the slain animals whose skins were used to clothe Adam and Eve to the slain Lamb of Revelation who is worshiped in glory and majesty, the cross is everything.

B. The Theme of Matthew's Gospel

Throughout his gospel Matthew successfully presents Jesus as king. But the end of Christ's life forced Matthew to accomplish something that might seem to be impossible: maintaining the majesty and dignity of Jesus Christ in the midst of His betrayal and execution. It is thrilling to see that there is no diminishing of Christ's glory in the gospel of Matthew. In Matthew 26:17-30 Christ appears more majestic and sovereign than at any other time in the gospel. Beginning in chapter 26, Matthew unfolds the glorious events of the death and resurrection of Christ. Verse 17 begins a section where we see Christ preparing Himself for His death by partaking of His final Passover and then establishing the Lord's Supper.

Lesson

I. EXPERIENCING THE FINAL PASSOVER (vv. 17-25)

A. Setting the Time (vv. 17-19)

"On the first day of the feast of unleavened bread, the disciples came to Jesus, saying unto him, Where wilt thou that we prepare for thee to eat the passover? And he said, Go into the city to such a man, and say unto him, The Master saith, My time is at hand; I will keep the passover at thy house with my disciples. And the disciples did as Jesus had appointed them, and they made ready the passover."

1. The persistence

   The Lord was committed to keeping the Passover. Matthew 3:15 says that He came to fulfill all righteousness, which is the law of God. One element of the law of God was keeping the Passover. Luke 22:15 says Jesus had an intense desire to keep the Passover with His disciples.

The Feasts of Israel

The Jewish year was filled with special feasts, not unlike our own. We celebrate occasions such as Christmas, Thanksgiving, Good Friday, and Easter. And some churches celebrate other holy days throughout the year. The Jewish people were no different. They held commemorative celebrations and festivals, which were occasions for remembering God's work in the past.

1. The Feast of Pentecost (Weeks)

   Pentecost celebrated God's provision in the harvest of their crops.

2. The Feast of Tabernacles (Booths or Tents)

   The Feast of Tabernacles commemorated the Israelites' wandering in the wilderness, when they lived in tents. God provided for them by giving them food and water as He led them through the wilderness.

3. The Day of Atonement

   The Day of Atonement was highlighted by a sacrifice in the Holy of Holies. The high priest entered into the Holy of Holies once a year and sprinkled blood on the altar to atone for the sins of the nation for that year.

4. The Feast of Purim

   The Feast of Purim celebrated the deliverance of the people of Israel by Queen Esther. She intervened at a time when the Jewish race was threatened with being wiped out.

5. The Feast of Dedication (Hanukkah)

The Feast of Dedication, also called the Feast of Lights, commemorated the deliverance of Israel under the leadership of Judas Maccabaeus during the intertestamental period (about 167 B.C.).

6. The Feast of Trumpets

The Feast of Trumpets celebrated the new year.

7. The Feast of Unleavened Bread (Passover)

Both the Feast of Unleavened Bread and Passover are mentioned in Matthew 26:17. Combined, these were an eight-day festival. The Feast of Unleavened Bread lasted one week, from the fifteenth to the twenty-first of Nisan (called Abib before the Exile) as prescribed in the Old Testament (Lev. 23:5-6). Passover was celebrated the day before, on the fourteenth. Those two celebrations were so connected in the minds of the people that they often referred to the entire eight-day period as the Feast of Unleavened Bread or Passover.

2. The purpose

a) The significance of Passover

(1) The symbol of deliverance

Passover celebrated God's deliverance of Israel out of four hundred years' bondage in Egypt. In Exodus 7:8–12:36 God sends plagues on the Egyptians. The last plague was the death of the firstborn in every family in Egypt (Ex. 12:29-30). God told the people of Israel to kill a spotless lamb and put its blood on the doorposts and the lintels of their homes. When the angel of death came to kill all the firstborn, he would see the blood and pass over that house (Ex. 12:3-13). When the firstborn sons were killed, the Pharaoh sent Israel out of Egypt, and God ultimately delivered them. So the celebration of Passover commemorated the sacrificial lamb whose blood enabled Israel to escape the judgment of God. It became a symbol of Jesus, God's Passover Lamb, whose blood enables one to escape the eternal judgment of God.

Selecting the Passover Lamb

According to Exodus 12:3, the Passover lamb was to be selected on the tenth of Nisan. As I studied the book of Matthew, I discovered that Jesus entered the city of Jerusalem on Monday for several reasons. Entering Jerusalem on Monday fits the chronology of events better than a Sunday entrance. It also eliminates the problem of what has been called a silent Wednesday: if Christ entered Jerusalem on Sunday, then nothing happened on Wednesday of Passion Week—a possibility that's hard to imagine. But most significantly, Monday was the tenth of Nisan in the year A.D. 33, the year in which our Lord died. On that Monday everyone in Jerusalem selected the Passover lamb.

After the lamb was selected, it lived with the family until it was slaughtered. When it was slaughtered, it was like slaughtering a pet. This helped the people better understand the price of sin. If Jesus entered Jerusalem on that Monday, He entered as the Passover Lamb on the proper day. Christ fulfills the symbolism of the Passover lamb in every way.

(2) The slaughter of lambs

Josephus, a first-century Jewish historian, said that more than a quarter of a million lambs were slain at Passover; these had to be slaughtered within a two-hour period. There were probably two-and-a-half million people in Jerusalem for the celebration (*Wars* vi.9.3). The impact of such a slaughter is mind-boggling. A river of blood would have run from the back of the Temple down the slope into the Kidron Valley. It filled up a brook that ran toward Bethlehem.

The Passover was a dramatic time of year for the nation of Israel. The Israelites were reminded that innocent lambs had to die to atone for their sins.

12

None of those lambs could actually take away sin, but their death was a profound example. Thousands upon thousands of lambs were slaughtered for millions of people, yet combined they couldn't take away one sin. Hebrews 10:3, 14 tell us that in one sacrifice Jesus Christ did what all the lambs, goats, and bulls could never do—take away sin forever.

b) The significance of unleavened bread

Unleavened bread contained no yeast. When the Hebrew women made yeast bread, they removed a piece of dough before baking as a starter for the next batch. If they didn't use a starter, the bread wouldn't rise. When Israel came out of Egypt, God told the people not to take leavened bread because leaven represented influence. God was telling them that He didn't want them to take any part of their Egyptian life and implant it into their new life. He was delivering them from their past—starting a new people in a new land. The symbol of that was unleavened bread.

3. The preparation

Matthew 26:17 says that the preparation was on the first day of the eight-day Feast of Unleavened Bread. The disciples came to Jesus and asked, "Where wilt thou that we prepare for thee to eat the passover?" Mark 14:12 adds that was "when they killed the passover." That tells us specifically that the Passover lamb was sacrificed on the first of the eight days. Beforehand, each household had to rid itself of any leaven so there wouldn't be any in the house during the eight-day period (cf. Ex. 12:18-20). Only then could the Passover meal be eaten.

The Day of Christ's Crucifixion

Passover took place on the fourteenth of Nisan. From one year to the next it fell on a different day of the week. In the year our Lord was crucified, Passover fell on a Friday. We can be sure it was Friday because Mark 15:42 says, "It was the preparation, that is, the day before the sabbath." The Sabbath is Saturday. The Jewish people referred to Friday as the day of preparation because that was the day they prepared for the Sabbath. Since the people couldn't work or prepare meals on the Sabbath, the day before was important.

In John 19:14 we read that Jesus was being tried before Pilate on "the preparation of the passover." That was also the normal day of preparation for the Sabbath, which just happened to occur on the Passover that year. Verse 31 says, "The Jews, therefore, because it was the preparation, that the bodies should not remain upon the cross on the sabbath day (for that sabbath day was an high day) . . ." That's another text showing that Christ was crucified on Friday, the day before the Sabbath. Verse 42 says, "There laid they Jesus, therefore, because of the Jews' preparation day."

Jesus was crucified on Friday, either in A.D. 30 or A.D. 33. The fourteenth of Nisan fell on a Friday in those years. I lean toward A.D. 33 as the proper year for Christ's death based on the chronology of other events.

A Typical Preparation for the Passover

The people had many things to do in preparation for eating the Passover meal. They had to prepare the unleavened bread. A bowl of salt water was put on the Passover table to remind them of the tears they shed in slavery and the parting of the Red Sea. They prepared a mixture of bitter herbs, frequently made up of horseradish, chicory, endive, lettuce, and horehound. That was done to remind them of the bitterness of slavery and the bunch of hyssop with which the blood of the lamb had been spread on the lintel and doorposts. They also made a paste of crushed apples, dates, pomegranates, and nuts called the *charoseth*. It was into this sauce that they dipped the bread during the meal. It is best seen as symbolizing the clay and mud they used in making bricks in Egypt. They also would put sticks of cinnamon in the sauce, which reminded them of the straw they used in making the bricks. Four cups of wine were prepared to remind them of the covenant of God in Exodus 6:6-7, "I will bring you out from under the burdens of the Egyptians, and I will rid you out of their bondage, and I will redeem you with an outstretched arm, and with great judgments; and I will take you to me for a people, and I will be to you a God."

14

Most important, the lamb had to be slain during a specific two-hour interval. Exodus 12:6 says it had to be slain in the evening. The Hebrew text literally says "between the two evenings." The Jews recognized an early evening at three o'clock and a late evening around five o'clock. Josephus tells us that the lamb had to be slain between the ninth and the eleventh hour, which is between three and five in the afternoon (*Wars* vi.9.3). It had to be slain by the priests in the Temple court. When the people arrived home, they had to roast their lambs right away. Following sunset, sometime later in the evening, they ate the Passover meal (Ex. 12:8). According to Josephus, there had to be at least ten people assembled to partake of the paschal lamb (*Wars* vi.9.3).

a) The request of the disciples

The disciples knew they had to prepare the Passover meal in Jerusalem where the lamb was required to be slain, but they needed to know a specific location. All who were staying in the periphery of Jerusalem had to crowd into the city and find a place where they could eat the Passover and have room for at least ten people and as many as twenty. That meant every available room in the city was filled up. So the disciples had a legitimate question.

b) The response of Jesus

(1) The secret preparation

(*a*) The representatives of the Savior

i) The indefinite man

In Matthew 26:18 Jesus says, "Go into the city to such a man." The phrase "such a man" is the translation of the Greek word *deina*. The best way to translate it would be "Mr. So-and-so." It's a nondescript term to purposely be indefinite. Now with 2 million people milling around the city, it would be impossible for them to find someone named "So-and-so." It's as if Jesus was saying, "Go into the city and find

15

a man, but I'm not going to tell you who he is." We have two options in interpreting Jesus' intention. Either He didn't know who the man was, or He didn't want the disciples to know who the man was. But since Jesus knew everything, we must conclude that He did not want the disciples to know who the man was.

Fortunately for the disciples, Jesus gave them a clue. Mark 14:13 says, "Go into the city, and there shall meet you a man bearing a pitcher of water." It was uncommon for a man to carry a pitcher of water because the women usually did that chore. Once the disciples found the man, they were to follow him (Mark 14:13).

ii) The intimate disciples

Luke 22:8 says that the Lord sent only Peter and John into the city while the rest stayed with Him. There were several reasons for that. One was that only two people were allowed to accompany a lamb to the sacrifice. You can understand why that was when you consider that there were only two hours available to slaughter the lambs. The priests could not finish in time if everyone went to the Temple. Peter and John were also chosen because they were the intimate, trusted disciples of Christ.

(b) The reason for the secrecy

Why was Jesus secretive about the identity of the man and the location of his house? Matthew 26:16 says, "From that time he [Judas Iscariot] sought opportunity to betray him." Judas was looking for a quiet, secluded place away from the mob where he could turn Jesus over to the religious authorities. Jesus knew that if Judas were aware of where they were going to eat the Passover, that would be the perfect setting for the betrayal. Peter and John never came back that day. They left early in the day, and the rest of the disciples never saw them until that evening. By then it was too late for Judas to make a deal with the leaders.

Why did Jesus not allow Judas to betray Him before the Passover? Because it was essential that Jesus celebrate the Passover with His disciples. Jesus wanted to use the Passover as an example of His own death so that He could transform that Old Covenant celebration into a memorial to His death. In addition, Jesus still had much to teach the disciples—He wanted to give them the promise of His Holy Spirit.

(2) The significant obligation

In Matthew 26:18 Jesus tells Peter and John, "Say to him, The Master [Gk., *ha didaskalos*, "the teacher" or "the rabbi"] saith." The man probably was one of Jesus' followers. Perhaps Jesus had even made prior arrangements with him. Peter and John were to pass on the message: "My time [Gk., *kairos*, "a special time"] is at hand." The moment of Christ's death was imminent. Many times Jesus had said, "Mine hour has not yet come." But now He said, "My time is at hand." Then Jesus told Peter and John to tell the man, "I will keep the passover at thy house with my disciples" (v. 18). The form of "I will keep" is in prophetic (futuristic) present, which makes it an obligation. Jesus was obligated to keep the Passover at the man's house with His disciples. Jesus was on a divine mission in accordance with a divine timetable.

c) The reaction of the disciples

Matthew 26:19 says, "The disciples did as Jesus had appointed [commanded] them, and they made ready the passover." Peter and John went into town, found

17

the man carrying the pitcher of water, followed him into his house, and made the necessary preparations.

4. The problem

Notice that Matthew 26:17 says, "Where wilt thou that we prepare for thee to eat the passover?" Verse 19 says, "They made ready the passover." And verse 21 says, "As they did eat." Putting those three verses together we can assume they were eating the Passover meal. Mark 14:12, 14, 16 and Luke 22:7-8, 11-12 support that assumption. There is no doubt that they ate the Passover meal. But there are other problems debated over by Bible scholars.

a) The chronological discrepancy

On Thursday the disciples made preparations for the meal. That afternoon the lamb was killed, and later that night they ate the meal. Just before the meal Judas left them and went to the religious leaders to betray Jesus. After Jesus and His disciples withdrew to the Garden of Gethsemane, Jesus was captured by the soldiers. The dawn of Friday morning followed as He was brought to trial. After the Jewish leaders held their mock trial, John 18:28 says they led "Jesus from Caiaphas unto the hall of judgment; and it was early. And they themselves went not into the judgment hall, lest they should be defiled; but that they might eat the passover."

Now we are faced with a chronological problem. How could Jesus have eaten a Passover meal the night before when the Jewish leaders didn't want to be defiled because they had yet to eat the Passover? Some claim Jesus had a private Passover. That can't be true because the lambs could be slain only at the authorized time. The leaders certainly weren't late in eating it because they were extremely religious. In addition John 19:14 says, "It was the preparation of the passover," which you recall means it was Friday. So we know it was Friday, yet the Jewish leaders hadn't eaten the Passover. How do we resolve that?

b) The consistent proofs

We know Christ came to die as the Passover Lamb. Matthew 27:46 says that Jesus died (on Friday) at the ninth hour, which is 3:00 P.M. He died at the exact moment when the slaughter of the lambs began. First Corinthians 5:7 says, "Even Christ, our passover, is sacrificed for us."

Jesus died on the day and at the time the lambs were slaughtered to fulfill every prophecy to the letter. But how could He eat the Passover on Thursday night? We know it wasn't just another meal because Jesus insisted that it be eaten inside the city of Jerusalem. The gospel writers constantly refer to it as the Passover. Furthermore, it was unusual for Jewish people to have a meal at night. To recline at the table was unusual for anything other than a festival meal. In a normal meal the breaking of bread occurred at the beginning, not in the middle of the meal, as in this case. The use of red wine also was unusual. They sang a hymn when they were finished with the meal, which was true of the Passover. And when Judas left, the disciples thought that he was going to give money to the poor, which was a typical event at Passover. We can be sure they ate a Passover meal.

c) The contrasting reckonings

The answer to how we can account for Jesus and the disciples eating the Passover on a different day than the Jewish leaders is based on how days were reckoned. We reckon a day from midnight to midnight. The Jewish people reckoned their days differently. They had two options. A day could be calculated from sunset to sunset or from sunrise to sunrise. The normal routine was sunrise to sunrise, but certain festivals, special days, and the sabbath were reckoned from sunset to sunset.

(1) Sunset to sunset

Exodus 12:18 says the Feast of Unleavened Bread had to be celebrated from sunset to sunset on Nisan 14 to Nisan 21. The Day of Atonement and the weekly Sabbath also were reckoned from sunset to sunset. Leviticus 22:6 says that any uncleanness needed to be dealt with before sunset. Perhaps things were reckoned that way because the order of creation seems to have followed that pattern. Genesis 1:5 says, "The evening and the morning were the first day," which indicates that God reckoned from evening to evening.

(2) Sunrise to sunrise

The Jews reckoned from sunrise to sunrise as the normal calendar day. Although we reckon from midnight to midnight, we think of our day as beginning when we rise in the morning. Their day officially began in the morning. Matthew 28:1 says, "In the end of the sabbath . . . it began to dawn toward the first day of the week." The first day of the week began at dawn.

d) The critical calculations

Regarding the Passover we can see a sunrise to sunrise reckoning in Deuteronomy 16:4. Combining that with Exodus 12:18, the Passover day could be calculated from sunset to sunset or sunrise to sunrise. Josephus, who was a Pharisee living in Jesus' day, explained that the law of the Passover called for the Paschal lamb to be eaten during the night with nothing left for morning (*Antiquities* iii.10.5). The Talmud, the codification of Jewish law, says it had to be eaten by midnight, which seems to indicate that the new day began after sunset (*Pesahim* x.9; *Zebahim* v.8).

It is thought that the Galileans and Pharisees reckoned the Passover day from sunrise to sunrise, whereas the Judeans and Sadducees, who made up the ruling body in Jerusalem, reckoned it from sunset to sunset. The Talmud tells us that the Galileans would not work on the day of Passover because their day began at sunrise. The Judeans would work until midday because their Passover day didn't begin until sunset (*Pesahim* iv.5). So the Galileans and Pharisees calculated the beginning of Passover on Thursday morning. The Judeans and Sadducees didn't calculate the beginning of Passover until Thursday evening at sunset, running until Friday evening at sunset.

e) The convincing harmonization

Matthew 26:17 follows the Galilean reckoning, so Jesus and the disciples had to kill their lamb on Thursday and eat the Passover meal Thursday evening. The Judeans and Sadducees didn't begin their Passover day festivities until late on Thursday and wouldn't kill their lambs until the prescribed time of day on Friday. That harmonizes John 18:28 with the other gospels.

Jesus had to die on Friday between three and five o'clock because that's when the Judean Passover lambs would be killed. But He also had to keep the Passover to transform it into the Lord's Supper. How could Jesus keep the Passover and still be the Passover lamb? Only if God allowed the two options for reckoning days to take place in history. When it came time for Jesus to die, there was no problem in having Him participate in the Galilean Passover on Thursday night and die during the Judean Passover on Friday afternoon.

Certainly the priest accommodated the two reckonings because it would be virtually impossible for all the lambs to be killed in one two-hour period. With the Galileans coming to the Temple on Thursday and the Judeans on Friday, at least the killing of the lambs could be divided into two days, and they could accomplish their task much more easily. Since it was difficult to find a room in Jerusalem to hold the Passover meal, it was convenient to double the capacity of the city by having two different days to eat the Passover.

Conclusion

God rules history and all tradition and customs to bring about the minute fulfillment of His perfect plan. Jesus had to keep the Passover to fulfill all righteousness, instruct His disciples, and give them a new memorial feast. Yet He had to die as the Passover Lamb. He did both because God controls history. We see Jesus Christ as anything but a victim. In three brief verses Matthew is able to present the majesty of Jesus Christ. This isn't something Jesus could have arranged on the weekend. It had to have been planned before the foundation of the world by the providence of God. Our Lord controlled every event on His path to the cross. None of His glory and dignity were lost in the midst of His betrayal.

Focusing on the Facts

1. What was the purpose of the life of Christ (see p. 8)?
2. Explain how the theme of sacrifice is revealed in both the Old and New Testaments (see pp. 8-9).
3. What feasts were celebrated by Israel? What was the significance of each (see pp. 10-11)?
4. What does the Passover symbolize? Explain (see pp. 11-12).
5. How did Christ's entrance into Jerusalem on Monday symbolize the Passover lamb (see p. 12)?
6. About what did the Passover remind the nation of Israel (see p. 12)?
7. Explain the significance of unleavened bread (see p. 13).
8. On what day of the week was Christ crucified? How can we be sure (see pp. 13-14)?
9. What did the people have to do in preparation for the Passover? What do the different preparations represent (see pp. 14-15)?
10. Why did the disciples need to know where they were going to eat the Passover (see p. 15)?
11. Why did Jesus send only Peter and John into Jerusalem (see p. 16)?
12. Why was Jesus secretive about where they would eat the Passover (see pp. 16-17)?
13. What is significant about the phrase "I will keep" in Matthew 26:18 (see p. 17)?

14. Define the problem raised by John 18:28 (see p. 18).
15. How can we be sure that Christ and His disciples did in fact eat the Passover meal (see p. 19)?
16. How did the Jewish people reckon their days? Explain (see pp. 19-20).
17. Explain how Jesus could eat the Passover with His disciples yet die as the Passover Lamb the next day (see p. 21).

Pondering the Principles

1. What does the sacrifice of Christ mean to you? If Christ's death is the focal point of all redemptive history, how does that affect you? Thank Christ for His willingness to offer Himself. Are you willing to make a sacrifice for someone else? List some specific things you might do. Now commit yourself to doing those things this week.

2. Read Hebrews 10:1-25. What do those verses teach about how sin is removed? Verses 19-25 detail how we should respond to what Christ has done. To what extent are you actively responding? Make a list of each response you should have. You may want to carry it in your Bible. At the end of each day this week, record next to each response how you fulfilled each one. Challenge yourself to pursue ways in which you can fulfill the role God wants you to perform.

2
The Last Passover—Part 2

Outline

Review
I. Experiencing the Last Passover (vv. 17-25)
  A. Setting the Time (vv. 17-19)

Lesson
  B. Sharing the Table (vv. 20-21a)
    1. Reclining at the table (v. 20)
    2. Proceeding through the meal (v. 21)
      a) The first cup of red wine
      b) The washing of hands
        (1) The argument
        (2) The rebuke
      c) The bitter herbs
      d) The second cup of red wine
      e) The unleavened bread
      f) The lamb
  C. Shocking the Twelve (vv. 21b-24)
    1. The shocking announcement (v. 21b)
    2. The sincere disciples (v. 22)
      a) Their sorrowful demeanor (v. 22a)
      b) Their wholesome distrust (v. 22b)
    3. The symbolic revelation (v. 23)
    4. The sovereign plan (v. 24a)
    5. The severe curse (v. 24b-c)
      a) The announcement of the curse (v. 24b)
      b) The application of the curse (v. 24c)

D. Signifying the Traitor (v. 25)
   1. Masquerading the truth (v. 25a)
   2. Confirming the truth (v. 25b)
      a) A special proof
      b) A satanic possession
II. Establishing the Future Provision (vv. 26-30)
   A. The Directives (vv. 26a-b, 27)
      1. Sharing the bread (v. 26)
      2. Sharing the cup (v. 27)
   B. The Doctrine (vv. 26c, 28)
      1. Of the bread (v. 26c)
         a) The old symbol
         b) The new symbol
      2. Of the blood (v. 28)
         a) The old requirement
         b) The new redemption
   C. The Duration (vv. 29-30)
      1. The future celebration (v. 29)
      2. The final hymn (v. 30)

Review

I. EXPERIENCING THE LAST PASSOVER (vv. 17-25)

A. Setting the Time (vv. 17-19; see pp. 9-22)

Lesson

B. Sharing the Table (vv. 20-21a)

1. Reclining at the table (v. 20)

"When the evening was come, he sat down with the twelve."

That's all Matthew says about the actual Passover meal, or Paschal meal, as it was often called. It was now after 6:00 P.M. on Thursday. Later in the night Christ would be captured and brought to a mock trial early in the morning. Then He would be crucified and die around 3:00 P.M.

on Friday. Christ and His disciples had to eat the Passover meal Thursday night before midnight, and nothing could be left in the morning.

Verse 20 says Jesus "sat down" or reclined. When God initially establishes the Passover in Exodus 12:11 He says, "Thus shall ye eat it: with your loins girded, your shoes on your feet, and your staff in your hand; and ye shall eat it in haste." But through the years the feast had developed into a more leisurely custom since there was no need to eat in haste, as the Israelites did the first time in preparation to leave Egypt. They adopted the custom of reclining when they ate the Passover, as they did for other feasts.

2. Proceeding through the meal (v. 21)

"As they did eat."

That takes us into the Passover meal itself. There was a defined sequence in the meal.

a) The first cup of red wine

The first thing they did was say a blessing and then drink the first of four cups of red wine. It was customary to mix the wine with water so that the participants would not get drunk. In fact, they used a double amount of water lest they should desecrate such a sacred occasion by becoming intoxicated. That first cup of wine was accompanied by a blessing (Luke 22:17), which symbolized the blessing of God.

b) The washing of hands

This ceremonial cleansing symbolized the participants' need for personal cleansing before they could eat the meal. Since they were celebrating God's salvation, they wanted to be sure there was nothing unclean in them. How could they celebrate the saving work of God while entertaining the sin from which He had saved them?

(1) The argument

It is likely that at this natural interlude in the feast, the conversation of the disciples turned to a familiar theme. Luke 22:24 says, "There was also strife among them, which of them should be accounted the greatest." While they were washing their hands as a sign of their inward cleansing, their souls were filled with pride and self-serving ambition. There was no connection between what they were doing on the outside and what they were doing in the inside. That is not unlike the many people who come to the Lord's Table and go through the motions while entertaining sin in their lives.

(2) The rebuke

At this particular time, Jesus realized their need to have their feet washed (John 13:1-5). If the washing of the hands was symbolic, the washing of the feet was practical, especially if you were reclining at a meal and your head was only a few inches from someone else's feet! In those days the people wore sandals, which didn't keep off much of anything, so their feet were either muddy or dusty. It was a common custom to wash one's feet whenever entering a home. But in the case of the disciples in the upper room, no servant had washed their feet. And certainly none of the disciples would stoop to do it, because they were arguing about who was the greatest.

No one was willing to take the role of a servant and disqualify himself from greatness. I believe it was at that time that Jesus "rose from supper, and laid aside his garments, and took a towel, and girded himself. After that he poureth water into a basin, and began to wash the disciples' feet" (John 13:4-5). Jesus gave them a profound lesson on humility and condescending love—on meeting the needs of others by taking the role of a slave. When Jesus was finished He said, "If I, then, your Lord and Master, have washed your feet, ye also ought to wash one another's feet" (v. 14). That lesson on humility was a strong rebuke to their pride, but Jesus also gave them a verbal rebuke for their pride (Luke 22:25-27). So the disciples were fully confronted with their sin before they got any further in the meal.

c) The bitter herbs

The bitter herbs were symbolic of the bitterness of bondage in Egypt. They were first dipped into salt water or vinegar.

d) The second cup of red wine

When the father or head of the table—in this case the Lord Himself—held the second cup, he instructed the present company on the meaning of the Passover meal. The participants then sang from the *Hallel*, from which the English word *hallelujah* originates. It means "praise" and is composed of Psalms 113-18. At this point in the meal they would sing Psalms 113-14 and then drink the second cup of wine.

e) The unleavened bread

The participants washed their hands a second time as a sign of respect for the bread they were about to eat. The host combined it with bitter herbs and dipped them in a sweet apple and nut sauce called *charoseth*, which was then passed to the guests.

f) The lamb

The lamb was then brought out. This was the major part of the meal. Dipping the bitter herbs and unleavened bread into the *charoseth* prior to eating the lamb was like an appetizer. Sometimes all three were combined together and dipped in the sauce. This is probably the *sop* mentioned in John 13:26-27.

C. Shocking the Twelve (vv. 21b-24)

1. The shocking announcement (v. 21b)

"[Jesus] said, Verily I say unto you that one of you shall betray me."

The translators used "betray" because Judas was a betrayer, but the Greek text literally reads, "One of you will deliver Me up." What a shocking announcement! When anyone shared a meal with another person in that part of the world and at that time in history, he was identifying himself as a friend. The idea of eating a meal with someone and then turning him over to his executioners was unthinkable. In Psalm 55:12-14 David contemplates such a betrayal: "It was not an enemy that reproached me; then I could have borne it. Neither was it he that hated me that did magnify himself against me; then I would have hidden myself from him; but it was thou, a man mine equal, my guide, and my familiar friend. We took sweet counsel together, and walked into the house of God in company." David was betrayed by a friend, not an enemy. The same is true in Jesus' case. When Jesus told the disciples that one of them would deliver Him over, they knew that one of them actually would do so, since Jesus would tell the truth.

2. The sincere disciples (v. 22)

a) Their sorrowful demeanor (v. 22a)

"They were exceedingly sorrowful."

The phrase "they were exceedingly sorrowful" indicates the degree of their sadness and grief. Some may have cried. The parallel account in John 13:22 says, "Then the disciples looked one on another, doubting of whom he spoke." They didn't know whom Jesus was talking about. They didn't know it was Judas, because he was excellent at playing out his masquerade. The parallel account in Luke 22:23 says, "They began to inquire among themselves, which of them it was that should do this thing."

Judas was so adept at his hypocrisy that the rest of the disciples had chosen him to be their treasurer. They didn't have any doubt about his integrity—they trusted him with their resources, which were meager at best. Jesus never did anything to expose Judas in front of the disciples. If anything, Jesus did everything He could to pull Judas close to Him. Judas sat to Christ's left during the meal, a place of great honor, according to Jewish historian Alfred Edersheim (*The Life and Times of Jesus the Messiah* [Grand Rapids, Mich.: Eerdmans, 1980 reprint], 2:494). Jesus also dipped bread and gave it to Judas (John 13:26), another symbol of Judas's honored position at the meal.

b) Their wholesome distrust (v. 22*b*)

"Every one of them [began] to say unto him, Lord, is it I?"

Why would each of the disciples be so quick to imagine himself as the traitor? Since Christ had just rebuked them for their pride and ambition, they felt ashamed. And they were doubly ashamed when Jesus washed their feet. In fact, Peter told Jesus, "Thou shalt never wash my feet. Jesus answered him, If I wash thee not, thou hast no part with me" (John 13:8). After having been so soundly rebuked, the disciples were especially sensitive about their weaknesses. So it is not surprising that even they didn't trust themselves regarding their possibly betraying Jesus. That shows great integrity on the part of the disciples. They knew that deep down inside them was a sinful principle so ugly that it might lead them to betray the One they loved. Commentator William Hendriksen said they had a "wholesome self-distrust" (*The Gospel of Matthew* [Grand Rapids, Mich.: Baker, 1973], p. 905).

3. The symbolic revelation (v. 23)

"He answered and said, He that dippeth his hand with me in the dish, the same shall betray me."

Christ and His disciples had no knives or forks; they ate with their hands, dipping the bread, the herbs, and perhaps even the lamb. When Jesus said, "He that dippeth his hand with me in the dish," He could have been referring to any of the twelve because they all were dipping food into the dish. In John 13:18 Jesus quotes from Psalm 41:9, pointing out the incongruity of the betrayal, "He that eateth bread with me hath lifted up his heel against me." That refers to Ahithophel, who betrayed his friend David (2 Sam. 16:20-23). Ahithophel is a picture of Judas, the ultimate traitor. The parallel account in Luke 22:21 says, "The hand of him that betrayeth me is with me on the table."

4. The sovereign plan (v. 24*a*)

"The Son of man goeth as it is written of him."

Christ was not a victim of a plan gone wrong. His betrayal is exactly what God had prewritten in prophetic history. No one did anything to Christ that was not a direct and immediate fulfillment of God's eternal plan. That is why Revelation 13:8 refers to "the Lamb slain from the foundation of the world." In Acts 2:23 Peter says Jesus of Nazareth was "delivered by the determinate counsel and foreknowledge of God." That was the divine plan.

Judas was a betrayer, but he was a betrayer by choice. He rejected grace and the offer of salvation. He made his own choice, yet God in His marvelous sovereignty used Judas's betrayal to accomplish His holy purposes. An unholy man in the hand of a sovereign God accomplished a holy end. But that doesn't make Judas a good man. During my senior year in seminary, I wrote my thesis on Judas. I was amazed to find a number of books taking the position that Judas was a hero, who should be exalted. They claim Judas forced Jesus to the cross to fulfill prophecy. Some even believe Judas purposely planned the crucifixion of Christ so that the world could be redeemed. That's simply not what Scripture says.

5. The severe curse (v. 24*b-c*)

   a) The announcement of the curse (v. 24*b*)

   "Woe unto that man by whom the Son of man is [delivered over]!"

   The man who betrayed Christ is cursed. Jesus said he was a devil (John 6:70). John 12:6 says he was a thief. He loved money and sold Jesus for money. Judas had no desire to usher in the kingdom on Christ's terms. He had no desire for the salvation of the world.

   The Old Testament predicted that Christ would die on a cross. Psalm 22 and Isaiah 53 describe the crucifixion in minute detail. It was written that He would die on the cross for the sins of the world. Yet even though that was in the plan of God, the man who turned Jesus over is still a cursed man.

   b) The application of the curse (v. 24*c*)

   "It had been good for that man if he had not been born."

   It would have been better never to have been born than to endure what Judas would endure—existence in eternal hell. The degrees of punishment in hell are related to one's level of rejection: the more truth one understands and rejects, the greater one's punishment in hell. Therefore, the severest damnation in hell is reserved for Judas who, in the words of Hebrews 10:29, has "trodden under foot the Son of God, and hath counted the blood of the covenant, with which he was sanctified, an unholy thing." Judas rejected the very One he had walked with for three years.

Judas made his own choices, and they were the source of his own damnation. Yet the choices fit perfectly into the sovereign plan of God. God controls not only the good but also the evil of man to accomplish His own ends. Jesus doesn't identify the betrayer in Matthew 26:24; He just pronounces damnation on him. However,

I believe He also gave Judas ample opportunity for salvation and repentance.

D. Signifying the Traitor (v. 25)

1. Masquerading the truth (v. 25a)

"Then Judas, who betrayed him, answered and said, Master, is it I?"

Judas had to say that. If he had said nothing, he would have been unmasked. He had to play the game. Everyone else asked Jesus that question, so he had to say it. He continued to masquerade his hypocrisy—as if he could hide anything from Christ. He called Jesus *ha didaskalos*, which means "master" or "teacher"—an aspect of Christ's life he was no more committed to than any other. All he wanted was money and glory.

2. Confirming the truth (v. 25b)

"[Jesus] said unto him, Thou hast said."

a) A special proof

John 13:24 tells us that at that particular moment Peter leaned over to John, who was on the right side of Jesus, and told John to ask the Lord who the betrayer was. Apparently Peter didn't hear the discussion of Matthew 26:25 between Judas and Jesus. So John said, "Lord, Who is it? Jesus answered, He it is to whom I shall give a sop, when I have dipped it. And when he had dipped the sop, he gave it to Judas Iscariot" (John 13:25-26). At that point John knew who the betrayer was whereas the rest did not.

b) A satanic possession

John 13:27 reveals the most frightful thing that ever happened in the life of Judas: "After the sop Satan entered into [Judas]." Satan himself entered Judas, who had just become a supreme agent of the fallen angel Lucifer in working against Jesus Christ. Although anyone who rejects Christ becomes a victim of Satan in that he unknowingly serves him (cf. Acts 26:18), Judas became a victim in the unique sense that he was indwelt by Satan.

In John 13:27 Jesus tells Judas, "What thou doest, do quickly." Verses 28-29 say, "Now no man at the table knew for what intent he spoke this unto him. For some of them thought, because Judas had the bag, that Jesus had said unto him, Buy those things that we have need of for the feast; or, that he should give something to the poor." Jesus got rid of Judas before they actually ate the meal because he was to have no part in the Lord's Table.

Why was this celebration of the Passover the final one? Passover was the oldest Jewish institution, with the exception of the Sabbath. For nearly 1,500 years the Jewish people had celebrated Passover. God instituted Passover before the Aaronic priesthood, before the Levitical rituals, and before the giving of the Mosaic law. But this Passover was the last divinely sanctioned Passover. Any Passover celebrated after this one is not authorized by God. It is a remnant of a covenant that has been replaced. Jesus celebrated this Passover to bring it to its end and begin a new memorial feast. This new feast is not of the Old Covenant but of the New. It was not initiated by the sacrifice of a lamb in Egypt but by the Lamb of God on Calvary. So Jesus ended the old before He began the new.

II. ESTABLISHING THE FUTURE PROVISION (vv. 26-30)

After having drawn the curtain on the Passover, Christ instituted the new feast. I want you to see three things: the directives, the doctrine, and the duration.

A. The Directives (vv. 26a-b, 27)

1. Sharing the bread (v. 26)

"As they were eating, Jesus took bread, and blessed it [gave thanks], and broke it, and gave it to the disciples, and said, Take, eat."

We don't know exactly at what point the breaking of the bread took place, but the phrase "as they were eating" tells us it could have happened just prior to eating the roasted Passover lamb or concurrently with it. Implied in Jesus' blessing (the direct object *it* does not appear in the Greek text) is His thanking God for the provision of bread (cf. 1 Tim. 4:4) and for the provision of His delivering power.

Jesus broke the bread because it came in large flat pieces, which had to be broken to be distributed. There's no symbolism intended in the breaking although some refer to the King James Version's mention of Christ's broken body (1 Cor. 11:24). However, His body was not broken. John 19:36 says that Christ's crucifixion fulfilled Scripture concerning the Messiah: "A bone of him shall not be broken." (See discussion on p. 61.)

2. Sharing the cup (v. 27)

"He took the cup, and gave thanks, and gave it to them, saying, Drink ye all of it."

The Greek word translated "gave thanks" is *eucharisteō*, from which we get the word *eucharist,* meaning "to give thanks" or "to bless." This was the third cup of the Passover, which was called "the cup of blessing." In 1 Corinthians 10:16 Paul says, "The cup of blessing which we bless, is it not the communion of the blood of Christ?" In 1 Corinthians 10:21 Paul calls it "the cup of the Lord." So the cup of blessing in the Passover became the cup of the Lord in this new celebration.

Mark 14:23 tells us that all eleven disciples shared the cup. Similarly, all of us who come to the Lord's Supper are participants. For many years in the Roman Catholic church only the priest drank from the cup. That's foreign to the intent of Scripture. All of us participate in the death and resurrection of Christ, and all of us are partakers of His supper.

B. The Doctrine (vv. 26c, 28)

1. Of the bread (v. 26c)

"This is my body."

a) The old symbol

That was a new concept. The unleavened bread had always been a symbol of leaving Egypt and the past life behind. Leaven symbolized influence, and the unleavened bread was a way of saying, "We're starting anew. Our old life will not influence us."

b) The new symbol

But now the unleavened bread symbolizes Christ's body. Luke 22:19 tells us Christ's complete sentence: "This is my body which is given for you; this do in remembrance of me" (cf. 1 Cor. 11:24). Jesus transformed the Passover, and that required a great deal of authority. Some people believe Christ was referring to His literal body. But that is not what Jesus meant. When Jesus said, "I am the true vine" (John 15:1), He didn't mean He was growing in a field! It is merely symbolic of Christ's body—the reality of His life given in sacrifice for the forgiveness of sin.

2. Of the blood (v. 28)

"This is my blood of the new testament [covenant] which is shed for many for the remission of sins."

a) The old requirement

That is a quote from Exodus 24:8. Jesus is saying that when God made a covenant with man, He required blood. When God made covenants with Noah (Gen. 8:20), Abraham (Gen. 15:10), and Moses (Ex. 24:5-8), blood was shed. God required the shedding of blood in making covenants with men. When God brought about reconciliation with Himself, the price was blood. That let man know that a relationship to God would cost the blood of a sacrifice. Hebrews 9:22 says, "Without shedding of blood is no remission." A covenant with God always demanded more than simple death; the death had to be accompanied by the shedding of blood because the life of the flesh is in the blood (Lev. 17:11). The pouring out of blood by animal sacrifice—a graphic and painful demonstration of the loss of life—pointed to Christ, who would be the final sacrifice for reconciliation with God.

b) The new redemption

Jesus died to save us from our sin. But it wasn't enough for Him to die; His blood had to pour out through the wounds in His hands, feet, side, and the thorn marks in His head. The blood running out of Christ graphically demonstrated that life was flowing out of Him as He offered Himself as the final sacrifice for sin. So Jesus tells us that the importance of the cup is to remind believers of His blood, which was shed on their behalf. The Greek word translated "shed" (*ekchelō*) is the key to understanding Matthew 26:28. It means "gush," "pour out," or "spill." Obviously we were saved through Christ's death—there was nothing in the chemistry of His blood to save us—but His blood needed to be shed because the only kind of sacrifices God accepted were those whose blood had been shed.

Notice that Matthew 26:28 says Christ's blood was shed for many. It literally means "for the benefit of many." Who are "the many"? All who believe, both Jew and Gentile. It was shed not just for the nation of Israel. Then Jesus said it was shed "for the forgiveness of sins." His substitutionary death brought about forgiveness. That's why Jesus came.

Our Lord instituted a memorial to His death the night before it occurred. He headed to the cross to pour out His blood as a sacrifice for sin. He instituted the bread and the cup as a memorial that we might remember His sacrificial death on our behalf. None of the sacrificial animals of the Old Covenant could take away sin. Only the blood of Christ could do that.

C. The Duration (vv. 29-30)

How long are we to celebrate the Lord's Supper?

1. The future celebration (v. 29)

   "I say unto you, I will not drink henceforth of this fruit of the vine, until that day when I drink it new with you in my Father's kingdom."

   Jesus is saying to keep celebrating it until He shares it with us in the kingdom. Since He was giving the disciples tragic news about the pouring out of His blood, He injected the promise that He would come back one day and drink the cup with them in His kingdom. Thus verse 29 is a reaffirmation of His coming kingdom.

2. The final hymn (v. 30)

   "When they had sung an hymn, they went out into the Mount of Olives."

   They had already sung Psalms 113-14. They probably had sung Psalms 115-16. After the fourth cup they might have sung Psalms 117-18. Praising God was the last thing they did before going to the Mount of Olives.

Focusing on the Facts

1. Why did Jesus sit down at the Passover meal (see p. 27)?
2. Describe the sequence of the actual Passover meal (see pp. 27-29).
3. What probably began at the point in the Passover meal when the participants ceremonially washed their hands? How did Jesus respond (see pp. 28-29)?
4. What was significant about sharing a meal with someone in the Jewish culture of Jesus' day (see p. 30)?
5. What effect did Jesus' announcement that one of the disciples would betray Him have on the disciples (see p. 30)?
6. What is the disciples' question in Matthew 26:22? Why did they ask it (see p. 31)?
7. Why was Christ not a victim at the hand of His betrayer (see p. 32)?
8. What future did Judas assign himself by his choice to betray Christ (see p. 33)?

9. According to John 13:27, what frightful thing happened to Judas (see pp. 34-35)?

10. Why was the Passover celebrated the night before our Lord's death—the final, God-ordained Passover (see p. 35)?

11. What directives did Jesus give for participating in His new feast (see pp. 35-36)?

12. What is the cup of blessing (see p. 36)?

13. What does unleavened bread symbolize in the Lord's Supper (see p. 37)?

14. What did God require when He made a covenant with man? What did He require in the New Covenant He made with man (see pp. 37-38)?

15. How long are we to celebrate the Lord's Supper (see pp. 38-39)?

Pondering the Principles

1. We know from Luke 22:24 that the disciples argued over who would be the greatest in the kingdom when they were probably going through a ceremonial cleansing of their hands. At a time when they should have been dealing with their sin, they were filled with pride. Evaluate the pattern of your life, especially your attitude when you participate at the Lord's Supper. How often have you come without truly dealing with a certain sin in your life? Take this time to examine yourself. Ask God to search your innermost being and reveal your sin. When you have isolated that sin, determine what kind of effort you will exercise to turn from it. Remember, your power to deal with any sin is only as strong as your dependence on God in all areas of your life. Be faithful to constantly examine your life.

2. The purpose of the Lord's Supper is to remind us of what God has done for us in providing salvation in Christ. What have you learned about Christ's sacrifice on your behalf that has been especially meaningful to you? Do you thank God regularly for the ultimate victory over sin and death that He has provided in Christ? After meditating on Isaiah 53, Ephesians 1-2, and 1 John 4:7-11, consider what impact Christ's death should have on your life. Having died to sin, are you living unto righteousness (1 Pet. 2:24)? Do you see good works in your life (Eph. 2:10) as a response of your gratitude for what God has graciously accomplished for you?

3
The Celebration of the Lord's Supper—
Part 1

Outline

Introduction
A. The Historical Context
  1. The deliverance from slavery
  2. The deliverance from sin
    a) Instituted by Christ
    b) Observed by the church
      (1) The fellowship described
      (2) The frequency delineated
B. The Literary Context

Lesson
I. The Perversion of the Lord's Supper (vv. 18-22)
  A. The Report About the Divisions (v. 18)
  B. The Reason for the Divisions (v. 19)
  C. The Rebuke Regarding the Divisions (vv. 20-22)
    1. Invalid Communion (v. 20)
    2. Insensitive consumption (v. 21)
    3. Incontestable condemnation (v. 22)

Conclusion

Introduction

First Corinthians 11:17-34 is an important part of the New Testament because it deals with the celebration of the Lord's Supper, also referred to as the Lord's Table or Communion. That celebration along with baptism are the two significant ordinances within Protestant Christianity. The reason the church attaches so much significance to them is that they were both instituted and commanded by the Lord Jesus Christ. In fact, I believe so strongly in a Christian's obedience to those two practices that I believe a Christian should question his own commitment if he does not observe them. Sometimes we struggle to know exactly what God's will is on a certain issue, but these ordinances are clearly commanded as a vital part of Christian experience. They should not be taken lightly and certainly shouldn't be ignored.

A. The Historical Context

1. The deliverance from slavery

On the night before His death, our Lord Jesus Christ gathered with His disciples in the upper room to eat the Passover meal. Every year the Jewish people met together to celebrate the Passover, which was a special meal designed by God to commemorate the deliverance of Israel from Egypt. After Israel had been in bondage in Egypt for more than four hundred years, God would deliver them from Egypt and bring them to the land of Canaan, which was to be their own land, having been promised by God to their forefathers. He brought upon Egypt a series of plagues designed to free the nation from Pharaoh's clutches. It was only after the last plague —the death of the firstborn throughout the entire land of Egypt—that Pharaoh finally agreed to let the Israelites leave. The children of Israel protected themselves from the angel of death who took the lives of the firstborn by taking the blood of a slain lamb and applying it to the doorposts and lintels of their houses. Then they were to eat the roasted lamb along with some unleavened bread and bitter herbs as the Passover meal.

Whenever an Israelite participated in the annual Passover feast, he would remember that God delivered his nation out of bondage in Egypt. The Passover celebrated today still recalls that great historic deliverance but tragically misses the greater deliverance that it foreshadowed—the cross of Christ.

2. The deliverance from sin

   a) Instituted by Christ

   Jesus took that ancient feast and transformed it into a meal with new meaning when He instructed His disciples to drink of the cup and eat of the bread in remembrance of His death on their behalf. Therefore, Calvary has superseded the Exodus from Egypt as the greatest redemptive event in history. Christians don't recall the blood on the doorpost and the lintel but the blood shed at the cross. The Lord's Supper is a memorial that Christ Himself instituted. He became the ultimate fulfillment of deliverance from sin and death when He died on the cross and shed His blood.

   Mark 14:22-25 records the account of the Passover meal known as the Last Supper of our Lord: "As they did eat, Jesus took bread, and blessed, and broke it, and gave to them, and said, Take, eat; this is my body. And he took the cup, and when he had given thanks, he gave to them; and they all drank of it. And he said unto them, This is my blood of the new testament [or covenant], which is shed for many. Verily I say unto you, I will drink no more of the fruit of the vine, until the day that I drink it new in the kingdom of God." That incident is also recorded in Matthew 26:26-29 and Luke 22:17-20, alluded to in John 13:12-30, and commented on by Paul in 1 Corinthians 11:23-34.

   b) Observed by the church

   (1) The fellowship described

       The Lord's Supper became the normal celebration of the early church. Upon hearing Peter's message on the Day of Pentecost, many of the people in Jerusalem "were baptized; and the same day there were added unto them [who had already believed in Christ] about three thousand souls. And they continued steadfastly in the apostles' doctrine and fellowship, and in breaking of bread, and in prayers" (Acts 2:41-42). The early church was involved in four basic activities: teaching the revelation the apostles had received from God, ministering to believers, observing the Lord's Supper, and praying.

During the Jewish celebrations of Passover and Pentecost, many pilgrims would come to Jerusalem and live with other Jewish families. Many of those pilgrims were saved through Peter's preaching on the Day of Pentecost and chose to remain in the city. The Christian residents of the city therefore had to take care of the converted pilgrims who had no livelihood. For that reason it was necessary for the early church to share and sell their possessions for the benefit of those pilgrims (Acts 2:44-45). In the same way the needs of slaves who had been saved were also met. The sharing of possessions and meals became a unique expression of community in the early church.

The breaking of bread became synonymous with a fellowship meal. The early church incorporated the Communion established by Jesus into the end of their fellowship meals. Eventually that combination of a fellowship meal and Communion became known as a "love feast" (Gk., *agapē*; Jude 12).

The early church attached Communion to a common meal not only because the Lord Jesus had done so but because the Jewish people had always associated the Passover with a meal. The Gentiles likewise included a potluck meal (Gk., *eranos*) with their religious festivals. So the early church followed those Jewish and Gentile cultural patterns in combining a meal with the Lord's Supper.

(2) The frequency delineated

I'm convinced that the early church celebrated the Lord's Supper on a daily basis (cf. Acts 2:46). In fact, it is not unlikely that they may have had

Communion with every meal they ate. It was common in those days for fellowship to revolve around a table as people ate together. The host simply sat down, took a piece of bread, broke it, and that act initiated the meal.

Later in the life of the church the frequency of sharing a meal with Communion was reduced to a weekly pattern (Acts 20:7). When the church met together on the first day of the week, they would have a fellowship meal and Communion, followed by a sermon. The love feast, however, gradually faded away since it was a practice of the culture and not something instituted by the Lord or the apostles.

Since the Bible doesn't specify the frequency of observing the Lord's Supper or other particulars, it would be acceptable to observe it after any meal whether in the home or the church. The important point is that you obey what the Lord says and exercise the wonderful privilege of commemorating the death and anticipating the return of Christ.

B. The Literary Context

One of the abuses that had arisen in the church at Corinth involved the Lord's Supper. In fact the Corinthians contributed to the death of the love feast. They obliterated its meaning. They selfishly turned it into a drunken and gluttonous exercise that resembled the idolatrous feasts they once participated in. Their practice was so offensive to God that He disciplined some of the Corinthians with illness and death (1 Cor. 11:29-30).

Christianity had broken down socio-economic barriers, yet within twenty years of Jesus' ascension, the Corinthians were starting to put them up again. The well-to-do were supposed to bring the food to the love feast and share it with the poor. But the rich would arrive early and eat all their food in their exclusive groups before the poor arrived, who then ended up going home hungry. In 1 Corinthians 11:33-34 Paul admonishes the Corinthians who were guilty:

"My brethren, when ye come together to eat, tarry one for another. And if any man hunger, let him eat at home, that ye come not together unto judgment." They had missed the purpose of the love feast, which was to share with others. Such an abuse of Christian love and unity made the participation in the Lord's Table that followed a mockery. Their selfish and divisive actions were irreconcilable with the grace and unity made available through the cross (Eph. 2:4-16) and the impartiality of God's love (Acts 10:34).

In chapter 11 Paul seeks to correct the Corinthians' abuses of the love feast and the Lord's Supper. Although he praises them in verse 2, Paul begins the section on the Lord's Supper with a rebuke in verse 17: "Now in this that I declare unto you I praise you not, that ye come together, not for the better but for the worse." The Greek word translated "declare" is *parangellō*, which means "to command authoritatively." Paul was telling them they would have been better off if they had stayed home. Their worship, instead of being helpful and edifying, was in fact destructive.

It is sad to say, but that condemnation is probably as applicable to many churches today, because either the people don't hear or apply the truth, or because they wrangle over personal preferences or trivial theological issues. When a church gets to the place where its meetings are for the worse, it's in trouble.

In the Corinthian assembly, the worst thing they could do for their spiritual growth was to get together. That's incredible in light of Hebrews 10:24-25: "Let us consider one other to provoke unto love and to good works, not forsaking the assembling of ourselves together." The only provoking the Corinthians did was to anger and selfishness. They had degraded the love feast and irreverently tacked the Lord's Supper on the end of it.

Lesson

I. THE PERVERSION OF THE LORD'S SUPPER (vv. 18-22)

A. The Report About the Divisions (v. 18)

"First of all, when ye come together in the church, I hear that there are divisions among you; and I partly believe it."

The Greek word translated "church" (*ekklēsia*) is never used in the New Testament to refer to a building but to an assembly of people. The Corinthian assembly of believers was characterized by divisions (Gk., *schismata*). That word refers to a difference of opinion. It is used in John 7:43 and John 9:16 of divisions that arose among the people over whether Jesus was sent from God or not.

Paul had heard more than once that there were differences of opinion among the Corinthians when they assembled. Instead of fellowshiping in a spirit of unity, they argued. They had already split the church on theological grounds over which leader to follow (1 Cor. 1:10-12). Now we learn of a social line of separation that had been drawn between rich and poor. That's why Paul said, "I beseech you, brethren, by the name of our Lord Jesus Christ, that ye all speak the same thing, and that there be no divisions among you, but that ye be perfectly joined together in the same mind and in the same judgment" (1 Cor. 1:10).

What causes a church to fight like that and split into factions? Paul gives us a clue in 1 Corinthians 3:1-3: "I, brethren, could not speak unto you as unto spiritual, but as unto carnal. . . . Ye are yet carnal; for whereas there is among you envying, and strife, and divisions, are ye not carnal and walk as men?" Carnality is pursuing the desires of the sinful flesh rather than being led by the Spirit to fulfill God's will.

Paul had heard reports of the spirit of divisiveness, which pervaded the Corinthian assembly like a raging fire. He may have believed they were somewhat exaggerated, so he mentioned that he couldn't fully believe them (v. 18).

B. The Reason for the Divisions (v. 19)

"There must be also heresies among you, that they who are approved may be made manifest among you."

Is Paul saying that the church has to have heresy? Yes, but not in the sense of false teaching. The English word *heresy* comes from a Greek root that speaks of a group's choosing and holding to an opinion. It's translated often in the gospels as "sect." It is used in a neutral sense in Acts 26:5 of the sect of the Pharisees. It's used in a negative sense in Galatians 5:20, where it refers to one of the works of the flesh—a self-centered factious clique.

Paul states that differences of opinions in the church are necessary by using the Greek word *dei* ("there must be" or "it is necessary"). That commonly used word often indicates something that is necessary because of the will of God. It was used in Luke 9:22 to convey that Jesus must suffer, die, and rise again. Heresies are necessary because God uses them in accomplishing His will: when problems and factions arise, "they who are approved" (Gk., *dokimoi*) are tested and found to be good. The Greek word for "approved" is used of metals that are refined by fire.

In a sense, evil is necessary to manifest good. You don't know who the peacemakers are in your church until you need someone to make peace. Adversity and contention cause the qualities of leadership, godliness, and being led by the Spirit to become visible in the lives of believers. Trouble has a way of manifesting personality and spirituality. The "approved" are those who persevere and give evidence of walking in the Spirit in the midst of a difficult situation.

First Thessalonians 2:4 tells us that Christians are tested, or approved, of God. They are the ones to whom Christ entrusts His ministry. Likewise, it is to such tested believers that church leaders should entrust the church ministries. Leaders can identify those who are approved by how they respond to difficulty and disagreements within the Body of Christ. I believe one reason some people become ineffective in their ministries is that they fail to stand the test of divinely-designed struggles. Consequently, they never reach the place where God will entrust the ministry of the gospel to them. Only those who pass the test of enduring temptation will be rewarded. James 1:12 says, "Blessed is the man that endureth temptation; for when he is tried [*dokimos*], he shall receive the crown of life." The approved Christian is one who goes through temptation and comes out victorious. He is the wheat among the tares (cf. Matt. 13:38). First John 2:19 says that unbelievers in the church can be identified when they depart from the faith: "They went out from us . . . that they might be made manifest that they were not all of us."

A church going through the process of purification will experience factions. Although factions may initially have the good result of enabling spiritually capable and responsible leaders to rise to the top, they become destructive if left unchallenged. That is why a factious person should be admonished twice and then put out of the church if he refuses to respond (Titus 3:10). The purity of the church is at stake.

Just in case you believe it would be a profitable ministry to develop leaders by creating problems, consider Luke 17:1-2, where Jesus says, "It is impossible but that offenses will come; but woe unto him, through whom they come! It were better for him that a millstone were hanged about his neck, and he cast into the sea, than that he should offend." Factions are going to happen—just don't be the one who causes them. The church is not to be a place where you stir up trouble.

C. The Rebuke Regarding the Divisions (vv. 20-22)

1. Invalid Communion (v. 20)

"When ye come together, therefore, into one place, this is not to eat the Lord's supper."

The factious Corinthian Christians had so corrupted the unity of fellowship that the love feast and Communion had become a mockery. The phrase "this is not to eat" could better be translated as "it is impossible to eat." They may have thought they were observing the Lord's Supper by breaking some bread, passing a cup, and saying some of Jesus' words, but those actions didn't make up for the spirit in which they conducted Communion. Their divisive and selfish hearts produced a superficial ceremony only.

2. Insensitive consumption (v. 21)

"In eating everyone taketh before the other his own supper; and one is hungry, and another is drunk."

Everyone knows that you don't come to a potluck and sit in a corner, eating your own food. But that's what the Corinthians were doing. The rich were gorging themselves and even getting drunk, while the poor had nothing to eat and remained hungry. This defeated the very purpose of the love feast and the Lord's Supper, which was to harmoniously meet the needs of the less fortunate and remember Christ's sacrifice that made them one. In place of the intended unity there was only selfish insensitivity to the needs of others. Clearly the Corinthians were not experiencing true communion with the Lord and among themselves by sharing the cup and the bread with one another (cf. 1 Cor. 10:16-17).

3. Incontestable condemnation (v. 22)

"What? Have ye not houses to eat and to drink in? Or despise ye the church of God, and shame them that have not? What shall I say to you? Shall I praise you in this? I praise you not."

In frustration, as if he were groping for a reason for the Corinthians' inappropriate behavior, Paul facetiously suggests that they didn't have houses in which to feed themselves. Certainly the group of Corinthians Paul was condemning wasn't roaming the streets to find food and coming to the love feast so that they could survive. If they wanted to selfishly indulge themselves, they could have done that at home.

Paul next suggested sarcastically that this group hated the church and would just as soon destroy it. It almost seemed as though the very thing Jesus had bought with His precious blood (1 Pet. 1:18-19), and was in the process of building (Matt. 16:18), the Corinthians were trying to destroy by sowing seeds of discord.

Finally, he suggested that maybe they wanted to shame the poor. The church is one place—maybe the only place —where rich and poor can commune together in mutual love and respect. Jesus and the apostles taught that (cf. John 13:34-35; James 2:1-9; 1 Pet. 4:8-10; 1 John 3:16-18). Unity through ministry to those in need and those among diverse groups became the pattern for the new church as they shared all things.

Although he knew that the Corinthians had homes and did not intend to destroy the church or shame the poor, Paul told them they were not deserving of any approval from him regarding their behavior at the love feast and the Lord's Supper.

Conclusion

Barriers among classes of people in the ancient world were rigid. There were clear separations between free men and slaves, men and women, those who spoke Greek and the barbarians who didn't, the educated and the uneducated, Jews and Gentiles, rich and poor, Roman citizens and those who weren't, and the cultured and the uncultured. But the church came along and shattered all those barriers, as Galatians 3:28 and Ephesians 2:14 indicate. The Corinthians were trying to put back up the very walls that Christ's death had broken down.

First Corinthians 11:17-22 shows us that we have an obligation to come to the Lord's Table. And when we gather together we must be sensitive to the needs of others, being careful that we not do anything that might cause division among fellow believers. There is no place for racial, social, sexual, or economic separations between believers in the church.

We come together to worship God and to celebrate our unity. Let our worship be pure and our unity be real. Rather than being like the Corinthians, may our fellowship be like that of the Thessalonians of whom Paul said, "We give thanks to God always for you all, making mention of you in our prayers, remembering without ceasing your work of faith, and labor of love, and patience of hope in our Lord Jesus Christ, in the sight of God and our Father. . . . As touching brotherly love, ye need not that I write unto you, for ye yourselves are taught of God to love one another" (1 Thess. 1:2-3; 4:9).

Focusing on the Facts

1. What are the two significant ordinances within Protestant Christianity? Why does the church attach so much significance to them (see p. 42)?
2. What was the Passover meal designed by God to commemorate (see p. 42)?
3. What kind of deliverance did Christ bring about, and how did He accomplish it (see p. 43)?
4. Identify the four basic activities in which the early church participated (Acts 2:41-42; see pp. 43-44).
5. Why did many pilgrims visiting Jerusalem on the Day of Pentecost choose to remain in the city? What was necessary for the Christian residents of the city to do (Acts 2:44-45; see p. 44)?
6. The combination of a fellowship meal with Communion became known as _____. Why was it not surprising for the early church to attach Communion to a meal (see p. 44)?
7. How often did the early church celebrate the Lord's Supper at first? How frequently did they celebrate it later (see pp. 44-45)?
8. Into what had the Corinthian church turned the Lord's Supper? What did God do as a result (see p. 45)?
9. How had the Corinthian church rebuilt the barriers that Christianity had broken down (see p. 45)?
10. What characterized the Corinthian assembly of believers? What social line of separation had they drawn (see p. 47)?
11. What causes a church to split into factions (see p. 47)?
12. Explain why heresies are necessary (see p. 48).
13. To whom does God entrust His ministry (see p. 48)?
14. Who will be rewarded, according to James 1:12 (see p. 49)?
15. According to Titus 3:10, how should a person who causes factions be challenged? Why (see p. 49)?
16. Were the Corinthian Christians actually observing the love feast and Communion? How were they defeating the purpose of those celebrations (see pp. 49-50)?

17. What became the pattern for ministry of the new church as they held all things in common (see p. 51)?
18. List the kinds of social barriers that existed in the ancient world. How were those barriers shattered? Support your answer with Scripture (see pp. 51-52).

Pondering the Principles

1. Do you make a point of participating in Communion every time it is offered at your church? Have you neglected that ordinance somewhat, or have you participated in the ceremony without focusing on the truth it is designed to highlight? Reread the different accounts of the Last Supper as well as Paul's commentary on it (Matt. 26:26-29; Mark 14:22-25; Luke 22:17-20; 1 Cor. 11:23-26). Are you remembering the Lord's death on your behalf, and are you looking forward to His return? Consider building a tradition of observing the Lord's Supper as a family or in a Bible study.

2. Do you fellowship regularly with other believers? Is your fellowship characterized by accountability for one another and a mutual love and respect? The church is a unique place where diverse kinds of people can rally around a common purpose—the worship of our Lord and Savior. Are you doing your part to build unity and harmony in your church? Are you being sensitive to the needs of believers around you? If your church doesn't already have a regular love feast, suggest that they have one with a view to meeting the needs of others and getting to know those with whom you will be spending eternity. Ask the Lord to deepen your love for one another so the testimony of your spirit of unity may be evident and attractive to the watching world (John 17:20-23).

4
The Celebration of the Lord's Supper—
Part 2

Outline

Introduction

Review
 I. The Perversion of the Lord's Supper (vv. 17-22)

Lesson
 II. The Purpose of the Lord's Supper (vv. 23-26)
   A. The Remembrance Requested (vv. 23-25)
     1. The source of the Supper (v. 23a)
     2. The setting of the Supper (v. 23b)
       a) The timing
         (1) The night of betrayal
         (2) The night of Passover
       b) The tradition
         (1) The first cup
         (2) The second cup
         (3) The third cup
         (4) The fourth cup
     3. The significance of the Supper (vv. 23c-25)
       a) The bread and the body (vv. 23c-24)
       b) The cup and the covenant (v. 25)
   B. The Propitiation Proclaimed (v. 26)
III. The Preparation for the Lord's Supper (vv. 27-34)
   A. The Conviction of Unworthy Communion (vv. 27-28)
     1. Analyzed (v. 27a)
     2. Applied (v. 27b)
     3. Avoided (v. 28)

Introduction

John 6:51-54 is an important passage that can help us better understand the Lord's Supper. It focuses on Christ presenting Himself to the Jewish people as the Bread of Life. In verse 51 Christ says, "I am the living bread that came down from heaven; if any man eat of this bread, he shall live forever; and the bread that I will give is my flesh, which I will give for the life of the world." That means that God the Son entered our world by taking on human form. He offers eternal life to those who receive Him in faith (symbolized by eating; John 1:12). Although He used physical terminology, He was conveying a spiritual message: receiving Him satisfies one's soul as eating bread satisfies one's stomach.

Jesus' statement confused some of those who heard Him: "The Jews, therefore, [argued] among themselves, saying, How can this man give us his flesh to eat? Then Jesus said unto them, Verily, verily, I say unto you, Except ye eat the flesh of the Son of man, and drink his blood, ye have no life in you. He who eateth my flesh, and drinketh my blood, hath eternal life; and I will raise him up at the last day. For my flesh is food indeed, and my blood is drink indeed. He that eateth my flesh, and drinketh my blood, dwelleth in me, and I in him" (vv. 52-56). These Jews were interpreting Jesus's metaphor in a literal, physical sense, but the Lord was speaking in a figurative way. He was saying they would need to acknowledge that He was God in human flesh and appropriate His sacrificial death on their behalf.

Unless you can accept the incarnation and the substitutionary, blood-atoning death of Christ on your behalf, you will never have eternal life. When you were saved you did that. And when you share in the bread and cup of Communion, you symbolize that spiritual appropriation. Communion is a restatement of our salvation and should also be a rededication of our faith. It's vital that we participate in it.

Review

The early church made a regular practice of celebrating the Lord's Supper as a memorial to the One who lived and died for them, as a time of communion with Him, as a proclamation of the meaning of the Lord's death, and as a sign of their anticipation of His return. The sacred and comprehensive nature of Communion behooves us to treat it with the dignity it deserves. That is precisely what the Corinthians did not do. They had turned the Lord's Supper into a mockery.

I. THE PERVERSION OF THE LORD'S SUPPER (vv. 17-22; see pp. 47-52)

Lesson

II. THE PURPOSE OF THE LORD'S SUPPER (vv. 23-26)

These verses are a beautiful presentation of the meaning of the Lord's Supper. The situation in Corinth was so vile that these verses are like a diamond dropped in a muddy road. Having preceded the passage with a rebuke of the church's failures and following it with a warning of chastisement, Paul drops this beautiful explanation in the midst of an irreverent and selfish background.

A. The Remembrance Requested (vv. 23-25)

1. The source of the Supper (v. 23a)

   "I have received of the Lord that which also I delivered unto you."

   What Paul had to say to the Corinthian Christians was not his own opinion. It wasn't a tradition that had been handed down from person to person; it was revelation he directly received from the Lord. In fact, most conservative Bible scholars agree that 1 Corinthians was probably written before any of the four gospels, which would make this passage the first divine revelation regarding the Lord's Supper.

2. The setting of the Supper (v. 23*b*)

"The Lord Jesus, the same night in which he was betrayed."

a) The timing

(1) The night of betrayal

Paul said that to set the historical context. He could have said, "on the eve of the Passover" or, "on Thursday night before the crucifixion." But in mentioning the betrayal of Jesus, he set the establishment of this beautiful ceremony against the background of something as ugly as the betrayal of Christ to heighten the contrast. In a similar way John 13, which records one of the most beautiful passages of love in the Bible, is interwoven with the account of Satan's entering Judas, who then went out and betrayed Jesus. And at the cross God the Son was surrounded by mockery and rejection while dying for the sins of the world. Such dark backgrounds make what Christ did all the more beautiful.

(2) The night of Passover

The night Jesus instituted the Lord's Supper was not an ordinary night. It had special significance since it was the Passover. Once a year the Jewish people celebrated Passover, which commemorated God's deliverance of the Israelites from Egypt. The Lord's Supper is the New Testament parallel to the Passover feast, because it celebrates God's delivering power, though in a greater way. We remember God's taking us out of bondage to sin into the kingdom of His dear Son (Col. 1:13).

This Passover was also significant because Jesus was crucified the next day while Passover was still being observed. As the Lamb of God, He was the ultimate Passover sacrifice (John 1:29; 1 Cor. 5:7).

b) The tradition

The Passover meal was structured around sharing four cups of wine at different intervals during the meal.

(1) The first cup

The Passover began when the host pronounced a blessing over the first cup, which was filled with red wine, symbolic of the blood of the lamb at the Passover in Egypt. That was followed by bitter herbs, which symbolized the bitterness of their bondage, and an explanation of the meaning of the Passover. The participants then sang Psalms 113 and 114 from a grouping of psalms called the *Hallel* (Heb., "praise").

(2) The second cup

After the second cup, the host would break unleavened bread, dip it into bitter herbs and a fruit sauce called *charoseth*, and share it with the participants in the meal. The unleavened bread symbolized the haste with which Israel was delivered out of Egypt. Then roasted lamb was brought out.

(3) The third cup

When the Passover meal was finished, the host prayed and then took the third cup. Then the participants sang the rest of the *Hallel* (Pss. 115-18).

It was the third cup following the meal that Jesus blessed and transformed into the Lord's Supper. Rather than remembering the physical deliverance of the Israelites from Egypt, the participants in Communion were to remember Christ's death and the deliverance it provided.

(4) The fourth cup

At the close of the meal, the participants enjoyed the fourth and final cup, which celebrated the coming kingdom. Mark 14:26 records the tradition of singing a closing hymn: "When [Jesus and the disciples] had sung an hymn, they went out to the Mount of Olives."

The Body and Blood of Christ

Jesus' identification of the wine and bread as His blood and body has been interpreted by the Roman Catholic church to be literal references to His physical blood and body. But that shows a misunderstanding of the meaning of the Greek verb *estin* ("to be"). The verb is frequently used to mean "represents." When Jesus said, "This is my body. . . . This cup is the new testament in my blood" (1 Cor. 11:24-25), He was saying that the bread and wine of that Passover meal represented His body and blood. The wine was not literally His blood; His blood was still in His veins when He said that. And the bread was not His body; His body was still present before all when He said that.

Jesus often spoke in figurative language. When He said, "I am the door" (John 10:9), He meant that He was the only channel through which people could enter into eternal life. He wasn't literally a door. The parables He told are examples of common things used to represent spiritual realities. The failure of some Jews to understand the figurative, metaphorical sense in which Jesus spoke of His body and blood caused them to stop following Him (John 6:53-66).

---

3. The significance of the Supper (vv. 23c-25)

   a) The bread and the body (vv. 23c-24)

   "The Lord Jesus . . . took bread; and when he had given thanks, he broke it, and said, Take, eat; this is my body which is broken for you: this do in remembrance of me."

"Had given thanks" is from the Greek verb *eucharisteō*. The English transliteration, Eucharist, is the name some people use to refer to the Lord's Supper.

The bread that had represented the Exodus now came to represent the body of the Lord. As the body to the Jewish mind represented the whole person, so the reference to Christ's body here symbolized His entire incarnation from His birth to His resurrection. Christ was born, crucified, and resurrected as a sacrificial gift given to mankind.

The Greek word translated "broken" doesn't appear in the better Greek manuscripts. The omission of that word is in keeping with John 19:33, 36. Those verses tell us that when soldiers came to break Jesus' legs (a common Roman practice to mercifully hasten the death of crucifixion victims), they noticed He was already dead and therefore didn't break them, thus fulfilling the Scripture, "A bone of him shall not be broken" (cf. Ps. 34:20; Ex. 12:46).

It Was for You

When Jesus said, "This is my body, which is for you," He was proclaiming that He was giving His life as the incarnate Son of God for you. The words "for you" reveal the unbelievably gracious sacrifice of God in sending His Son. He became a man for you, He suffered for you, and He died for you. Was it for Himself that He was subjected to the hatred and mockery of people who rejected Him and plotted His death? Why did He go to the Garden of Gethsemane, pouring out His heart in anguish, and choose to fulfill His Father's will? Was it for Himself? No. It was for you. What an magnanimous act of divine love! Even though you don't deserve it, He still gave His life for you. Whether you want to accept the sacrifice of Christ on your behalf is your choice, but that does not change the fact that His life was given for you. The benefit of Christ's death is offered to everyone since it paid for the sin of all men. And Christ still lives as a sympathetic high priest for you, who can identify with your suffering and offer divine comfort (Heb. 4:15-16). Not only did He die for you, but He rose and lives forevermore for you.

In response to all He has done for us, Christ asks us to remember Him and what He has accomplished. Partaking in Communion in not an option for believers; it is a command from the Lord Himself. To neglect the Lord's Supper is to be disobedient. Jesus didn't specify how often you should take Communion, but when your church offers it you should take it. That doesn't mean you can't observe it more often if you'd like. You can participate in Communion in your home, in a prayer group, or at a Bible study. The important thing is that you do it.

The concept of remembering to the Hebrew mind meant more than simply recalling something that happened in the past. It meant recapturing as much of the reality and significance of a person or situation as possible in one's conscious mind. Jesus was requesting that Christians ponder the meaning of His life and death on their behalf. A person can participate in Communion, but if his mind is a million miles away, he hasn't truly remembered the Lord.

b) The cup and the covenant (v. 25)

"After the same manner also he took the cup, when he had supped, saying, This cup is the new testament in my blood: this do, as often as ye drink it, in remembrance of me."

Taking the third cup of Passover after the meal had been finished, Jesus stated that the cup of wine represented the New Covenant (Gk., *diathēkē*), or promise, that would soon be ratified by His blood. The Old Covenant was ratified by the blood of animals, and the New Covenant was ratified by the blood of Christ. In the same way that a signature ratifies a contract or promise today, shedding the blood of a sacrificial animal ratified one in the Old Testament. God promised not to take the lives of the Israelites' firstborn and to lead them out of Egypt to the Promised Land if they would agree to sign on the dotted line, so to speak, with the blood of a lamb smeared on the doorposts and lintels of their homes. The practice of ratifying a covenant with the blood of an animal was common not only in the Old Testament but in most of the ancient Near East.

Whereas the Old Covenant required continual animal sacrifices, the New Covenant, represented by the cup of Communion, was fulfilled by the once-for-all sacrifice of the Lamb of God for the forgiveness of sins for all time (Heb. 9:28). It was as if on the cross Jesus was taking His blood and signing on the dotted line. It looked beyond the temporal blessings of the Old Covenant to the eternal blessings of the New Covenant. The blood of the Passover has been replaced by the blood of the cross. Every time we celebrate the Lord's Supper we are declaring God's provision of salvation and renewing our faith in Him.

B. The Propitiation Proclaimed (v. 26)

"As often as ye eat this bread, and drink this cup, ye do show the Lord's death till he come."

We proclaim the death of Christ every time we remember Him in Communion. The world is reminded that God became man and died a substitutionary sin-atoning death for all mankind (cf. 1 John 2:2). We also look forward to the day when we will commune with Him in His presence.

The Lord's Table is a comprehensive ordinance. We remember what Christ has done, we refresh our commitment to Him, we commune with Him, we proclaim the gospel, and we anticipate His return. That is why we must observe it with the right attitude.

III. THE PREPARATION FOR THE LORD'S SUPPER (vv. 27-34)

A. The Conviction of Unworthy Communion (vv. 27-28)

1. Analyzed (v. 27a)

"Wherefore, whosoever shall eat this bread, and drink this cup of the Lord, unworthily."

The Corinthians were partaking of Communion in an unworthy manner. We also can do this in any of several ways:

a) By ignoring it rather than obeying it. If we say Communion is irrelevant and unimportant, we are observing it unworthily.

b) By failing to observe it meaningfully. We can be concerned with going through the ritualistic motions without understanding the reason for observing it. Superficial ceremony and irreverence can prevent us from personally experiencing communion with Christ.

c) By assuming it can save. Taking Communion does not impart saving grace. It is the privilege of those who are already saved to confront their sin and renew their fellowship with Christ.

d) By refusing to confess and repent from sin. We should never participate in the Lord's Supper if we have unresolved bitterness toward another Christian or any unconfessed sin in our lives.

e) By having a lack of respect and love for God or His children.

2. Applied (v. 27b)

"Shall be guilty of the body and blood of the Lord."

The result of coming to the Lord's Supper unworthily is that one is treating Christ's unique life and death as something common and insignificant. A man who tramples on his nation's flag isn't merely trampling on a piece of cloth; he is guilty of dishonoring his country. Likewise, someone who tramples on the body and blood of Christ, as represented in the elements of Communion, is guilty of dishonoring Christ Himself. Communion is a real encounter with Christ. It's so real that failure to acknowledge the reality behind it brings about judgment (v. 29).

3. Avoided (v. 28)

"But let a man examine himself, and so let him eat of that bread, and drink of that cup."

The Greek word translated "examine" conveys the idea of a rigorous self-examination. Check out your life—your motives and your attitudes toward the Lord, His Supper, and other Christians. We need to be certain we're not careless, flippant, indifferent, unrepentant, or irreverent when we partake of Communion. We must examine our hearts to discover if there's anything that shouldn't be there. When we have examined ourselves and dealt with any sin or improper motive, then we are ready to share in the bread and the cup.

B. The Consequence of Unworthy Communion (vv. 29-32)

1. The cause of chastening (v. 29)

"He that eateth and drinketh unworthily, eateth and drinketh judgment to himself, not discerning the Lord's body."

The Greek word translated "judgment" is *krima* and is better translated "chastisement." It refers to the Lord's chastisement of believers, not the damnation of unbelievers, which is referred to in verse 32 with the Greek term *katakrinō*. A believer fails to discern the Lord's body when he disregards the reality of Christ in Communion and treats the ordinance with a lack of seriousness, dignity, or sacredness. Such a person has not discerned the meaning and significance of the Lord's body. Although a reference to the corporate body of Christ may be implied in this verse, the context supports a reference to the Lord Himself.

2. The results of chastening (vv. 30-31)

a) Administered (v. 30)

"For this cause many are weak and sickly among you, and many sleep."

The Lord disciplined the Corinthians' abuse of the Lord's Supper by causing some to be sick and by taking the lives of others. The Greek word translated "sleep" is a common New Testament metaphor for the death of believers (John 11:11; Acts 7:60; 1 Thess.

4:13-15). A number in Corinth had died for partaking of the Lord's Supper in an irreverent manner. In a similar way God put to death Ananias and Sapphira for lying to the Holy Spirit (Acts 5:1-11). Such stark reminders of God's holiness and man's sinfulness show what all men deserve and what some actually receive. Some Christians today have quite possibly become weak and sick or have died as a result of incorrectly observing the Lord's Supper.

b) Avoided (v. 31)

"If we would judge ourselves, we should not be judged."

Paul is saying that if we examine ourselves, we wouldn't end up being chastened. Instead of following the example of the Corinthians, who were chastened by God because they wouldn't examine themselves, we need to acknowledge and confess our sins and evaluate the purity of our motives as we take Communion.

3. The reason for chastening (v. 32)

"But when we are judged, we are chastened of the Lord, that we should not be condemned with the world."

At this point some Christians might hesitate coming to the Lord's Supper for fear of receiving divine punishment. However, Paul assures us that although we might be chastened by the Lord, we will not be damned with the world. No Christian under any circumstance will ever be damned with the world because he was chastened by the Lord. The Greek word translated "chastened" is used of a father's discipline of his child (cf. Eph. 6:4). God disciplines His children not to punish them but to correct their sinful behavior and direct them in the paths of righteousness. Hebrews 12:6 says, "Whom the Lord loveth he chasteneth, and scourgeth every son he receiveth." Every Christian is under the chastening hand of the Lord, which prevents him from ever being condemned with the world. So we don't have to fear losing our salvation and being eternally separated from the presence of God. God will intervene with His chastening hand before that can happen.

C. The Correction of Unworthy Communion (vv. 33-34)

"Wherefore, my brethren, when ye come together to eat, tarry one for another. And if any man hunger, let him eat at home, that ye come not together unto judgment. And the rest will I set in order when I come."

Paul instructs the Corinthians to wait for each other when they congregate for the love feast and the Lord's Supper rather than selfishly gorging themselves before the poor arrive. Those who were attending to satisfy their physical hunger were to eat at home. Otherwise they would pervert the purpose of the love feast and the Lord's Supper and would be subject to divine chastening.

I don't know what the rest of the problems were that the Corinthians had, but they were most likely related to matters of worship or remaining issues about the Lord's Supper that could be dealt with when he personally arrived in Corinth.

The Lord is serious about how the ordinance of Communion is to be treated. We must never overlook its significance or fail to evaluate our hearts before we partake of it.

Focusing on the Facts

1. What did Jesus mean by claiming to be the Bread of Life? How did those who heard Him interpret His statements (see p. 56)?
2. How is 1 Corinthians 11:23-26 like a diamond in a muddy road (see p. 57)?
3. Identify the source of Paul's instruction about the Lord's Supper (see p. 57).
4. Explain the significance of the Lord's Supper being instituted on the night of Jesus' betrayal and on Passover (see pp. 58-59).
5. How has Jesus' identification of the bread and wine as His body and blood been misinterpreted today? How can the Greek verb *estin* ("to be") also be translated (see p. 60)?

6. What does the reference to Christ's body (symbolized by the bread) represent (see p. 61)?

7. In response to all Christ has done for us, what did He ask us to do (see p. 62)?

8. Compare how the Old and New Covenants were ratified (see pp. 62-63)?

9. What do Christians silently proclaim when they participate in the Lord's Supper (see p. 63)?

10. List some ways in which a person could partake of Communion in an unworthy manner (see p. 64).

11. In what sense can a Christian be "guilty of the body and blood of the Lord" (1 Cor. 11:27; see p. 64)?

12. How can a Christian avoid dishonoring Christ in Communion (see p. 65)?

13. In what does failure to discern the significance of the Lord's sacrificial life and death result (1 Cor. 11:29; see p. 65)?

14. What kind of chastening did some of the Corinthians receive (1 Cor. 11:30; see pp. 65-66)?

15. What did Paul instruct the Corinthians to do to correct their abuses and prevent being judged (1 Cor. 11:31; see p. 66)?

16. Compare the chastening the believer receives with the judgment the unbeliever receives (1 Cor. 11:32; see p. 66).

Pondering the Principles

1. Do you have Jewish friends, neighbors, relatives, or coworkers who have not yet recognized Christ as the Jewish Messiah? Although this chapter touched upon some of the significance of the Passover that was fulfilled by Christ, there are other fascinating parallels. Find some study materials at a Christian bookstore, a church or Christian school library, or a ministry outreach to Jewish people that can help you prepare to show them how Christ has become their Passover Lamb.

2. Look over the variety of ways the Lord's Supper can be treated unworthily (see p. 64). Examining your life, do you find yourself guilty of anything on that list? If so, after confessing your sin to the Lord, what steps do you need to take to correct that situation? In 1 Corinthians 11 Paul tells us to examine ourselves (vv. 28, 31), discern the significance of the Lord's life and death (v. 29), and participate in the Lord's Supper for the right reasons (v. 34). With your family or a Christian friend, discuss how

you can highlight the importance of the next celebration of Communion. Consider reading appropriate passages of Scripture together, such as those about Christ's crucifixion or return.

3. Find out when your church will be celebrating Communion next and write the date on your calendar. Beforehand, ask the Lord to reveal any sin you have not yet confessed. During the service, fight any temptation to daydream. Make a conscious effort to ponder Christ's life and death on your behalf. Look upon Communion as you would a reunion with a close friend or relative. The unique spiritual encounter of a Christian with his living Lord and Savior is a reunion well worth preparing for.

Scripture Index

Topical Index